Disney characters and artwork © Disney Enterprises, Inc.

ISBN 978-0-634-06635-1

WALT DISNEY MUSIC COMPANY
WONDERLAND MUSIC COMPANY, INC.

DISTRIBUTED BY

HAL•LEONARD®
CORPORATION

7777 W. BLUEMOUND RD. P.O. BOX 13819 MILWAUKEE, WI 53213

In Australia Contact:
Hal Leonard Australia Pty. Ltd.
22 Taunton Drive P.O. Box 5130
Cheltenham East, 3192 Victoria, Australia
Email: ausadmin@halleonard.com

Visit Hal Leonard Online at
www.halleonard.com

Be Our Guest
from Walt Disney's BEAUTY AND THE BEAST

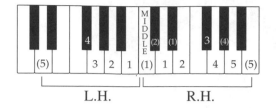

Lyrics by Howard Ashman
Music by Alan Menken

Brightly

Be our guest! Be our guest! Put our

serv - ice to the test. Tie our nap - kin 'round your

Duet Part (Student plays one octave higher than written.)

Brightly

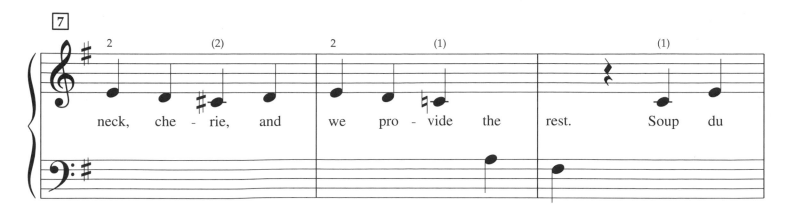

neck, che - rie, and we pro - vide the rest. Soup du

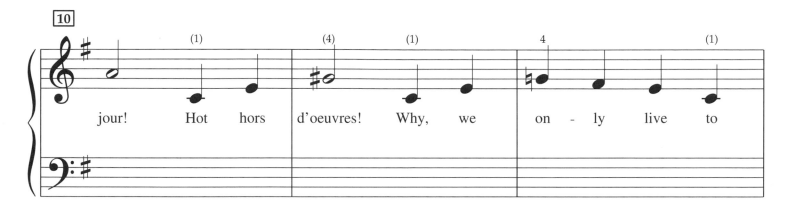

jour! Hot hors d'oeuvres! Why, we on - ly live to

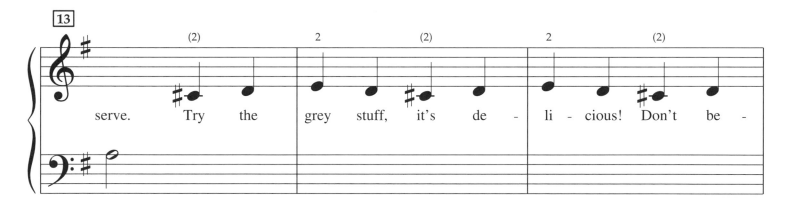

serve. Try the grey stuff, it's de - li - cious! Don't be -

lieve me? *(Spoken:) Ask the* dish - es! They can sing! They can

dance! *(Spoken:) Af* - *ter* *all,* *Miss,* *this* *is* *France!* And a

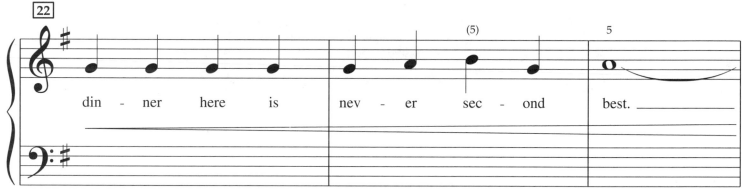

din - ner here is nev - er sec - ond best. _____

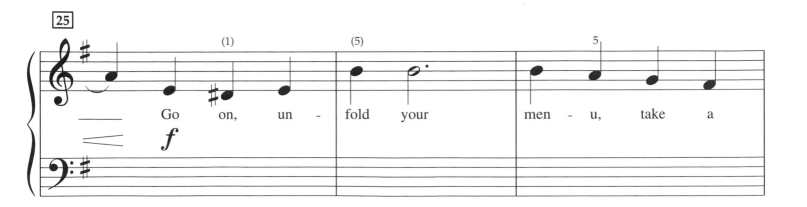

Go on, un - fold your men - u, take a

glance, and then you'll be our guest, *(Spoken:)* oui, our

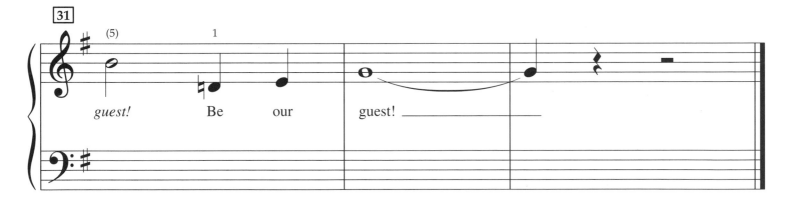

guest! Be our guest! _____

Can You Feel the Love Tonight

from Walt Disney Pictures' THE LION KING

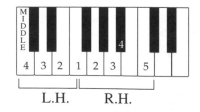

Music by Elton John
Lyrics by Tim Rice

Peacefully

Chorus: Can you feel the love to-night,

the peace the eve-ning brings? The world, for once, in per-fect har-mo-ny with

Duet Part (Student plays one octave higher than written.)

Peacefully

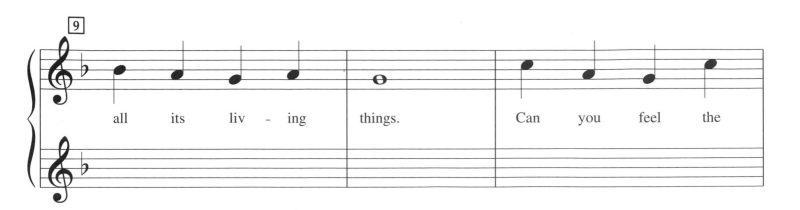

all its liv – ing things. Can you feel the

love to - night? You need-n't look too far.

Steal-ing through the night's un – cer - tain-ties, love is where they

If I Didn't Have You

Walt Disney Pictures Presents
A Pixar Animation Studios Film MONSTERS, INC.

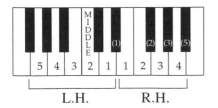

Music and Lyrics by
Randy Newman

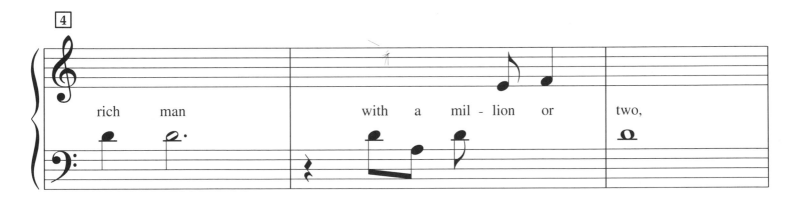

Duet Part (Student plays one octave higher than written.)

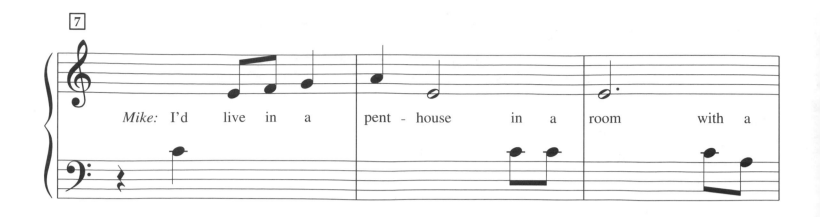

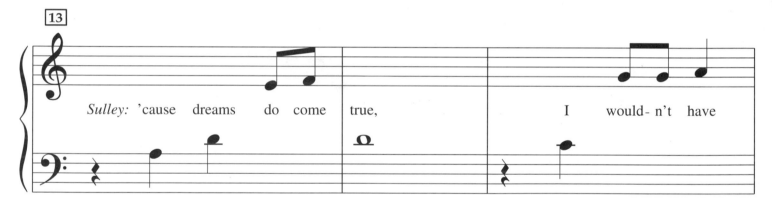

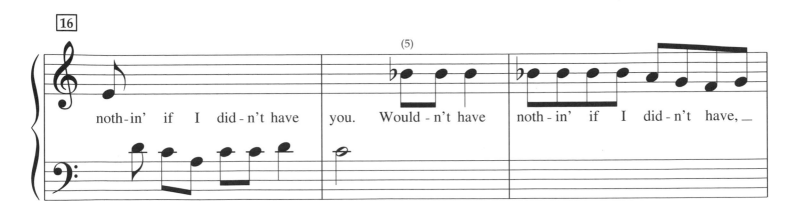

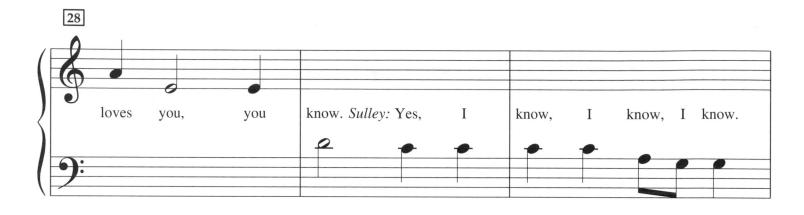

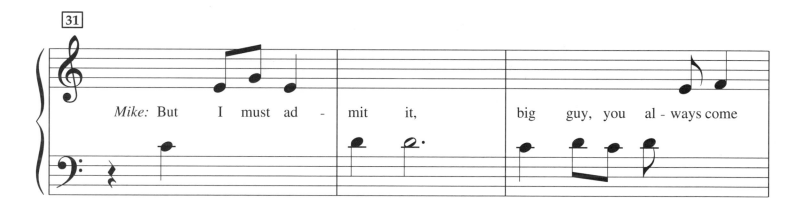

through.   I would - n't have   noth - ing if I did - n't have

(1)   1

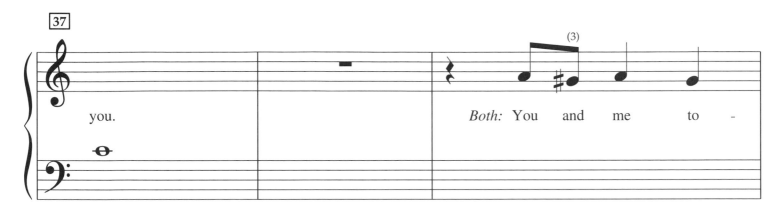

you.   *Both:* You   and   me   to   -

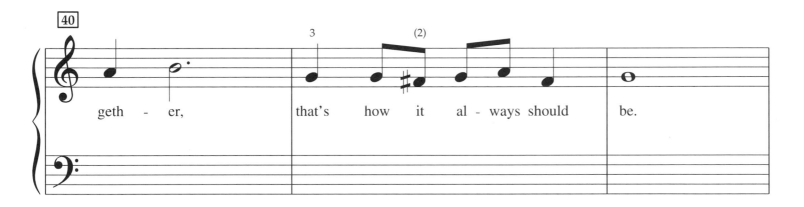

geth - er,   that's   how   it   al - ways should   be.

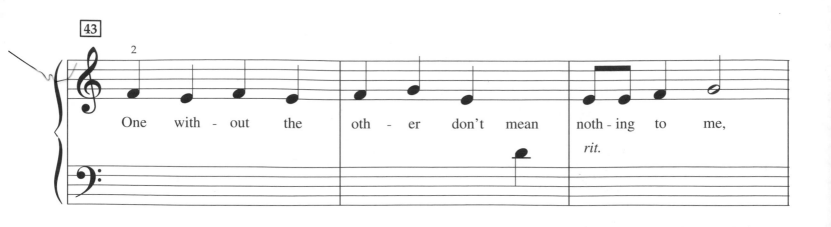

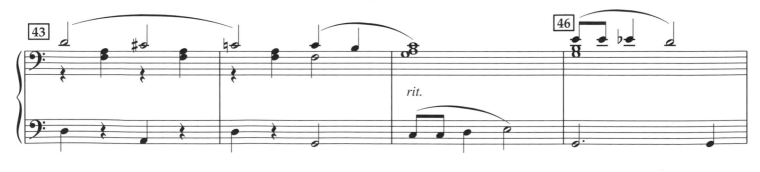

14

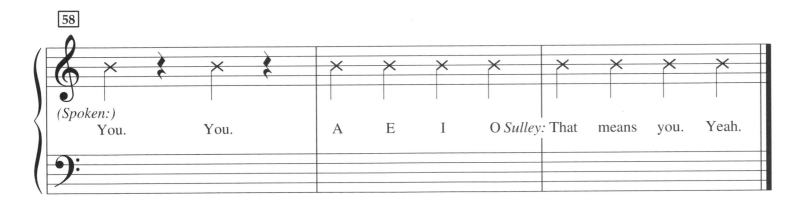

15

Kiss the Girl
from Walt Disney's THE LITTLE MERMAID

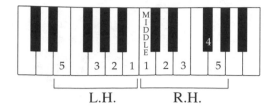

Lyrics by Howard Ashman
Music by Alan Menken

Moderately, with a steady beat

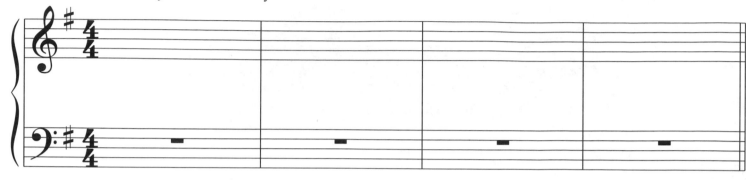

There you see her
Now's your

see her
mo - ment,

sit - ting there a - cross the
float - ing in a blue la -

Duet Part (Student plays one octave higher than written.)

Moderately, with a steady beat

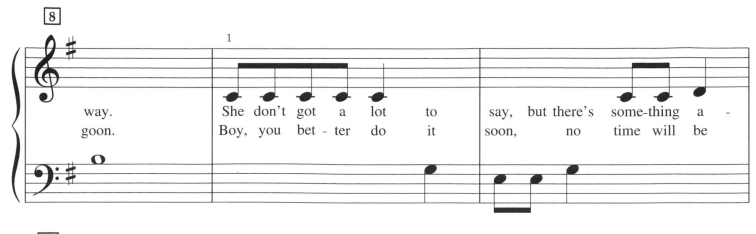

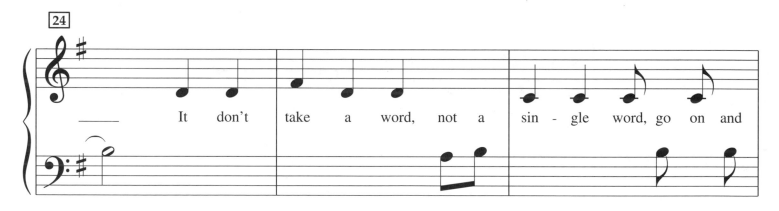

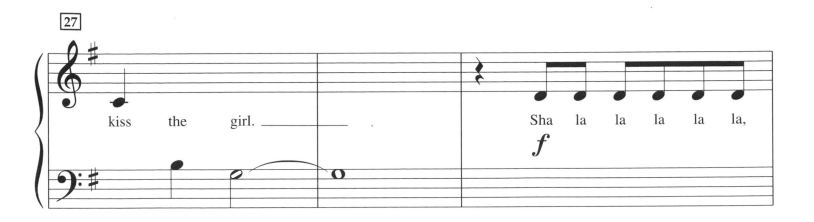

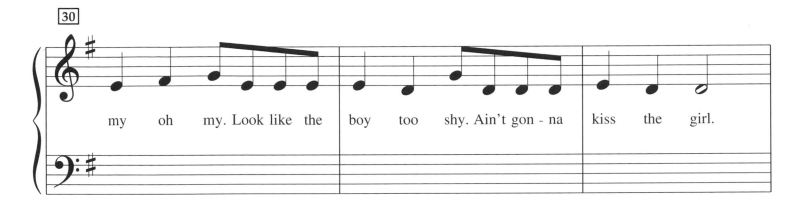

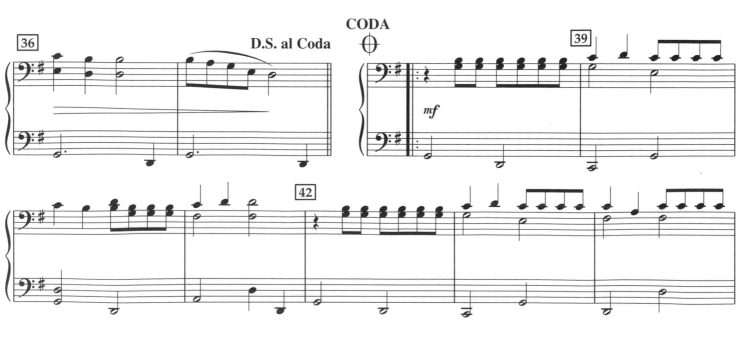

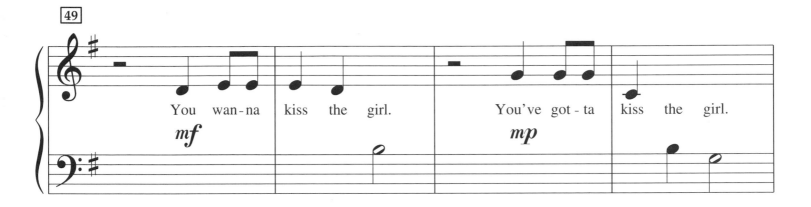

My Funny Friend and Me

from Walt Disney Pictures' THE EMPEROR'S NEW GROOVE

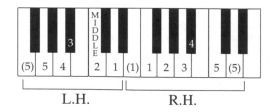

Lyrics by Sting
Music by Sting and David Hartley

Moderately, with expression

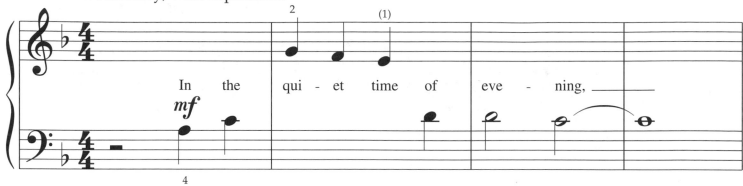

In the qui - et time of eve - ning, when the stars as - sume their pat - terns

Duet Part (Student plays one octave higher than written.)

Moderately, with expression

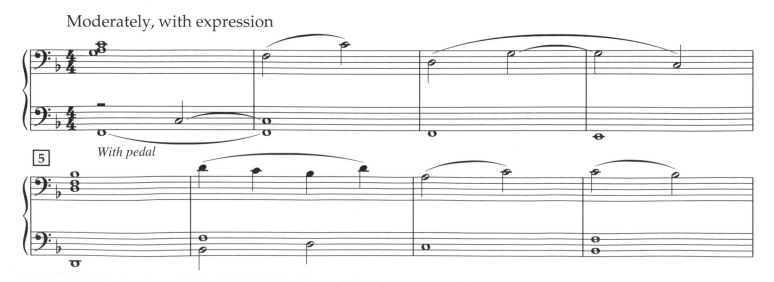

With pedal

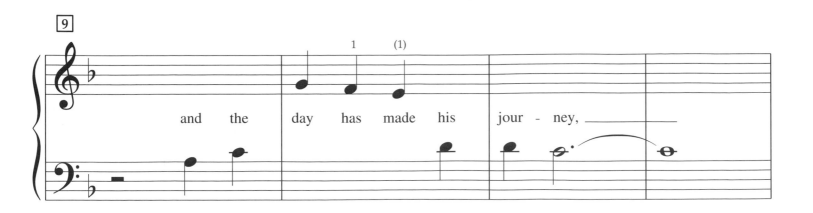

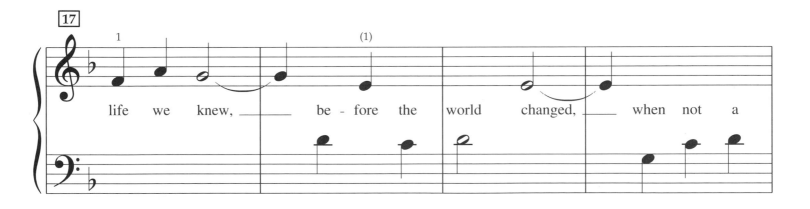

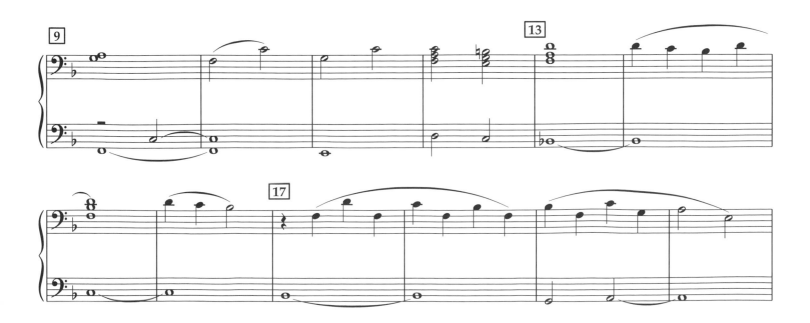

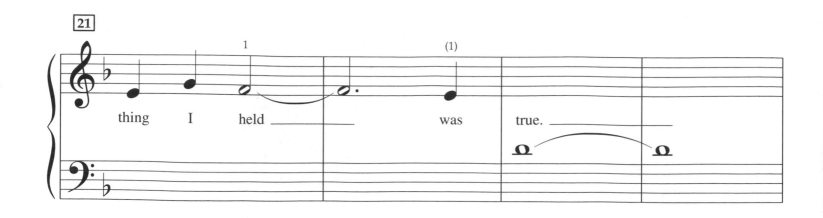

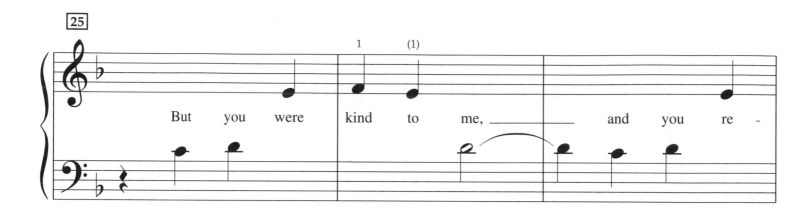

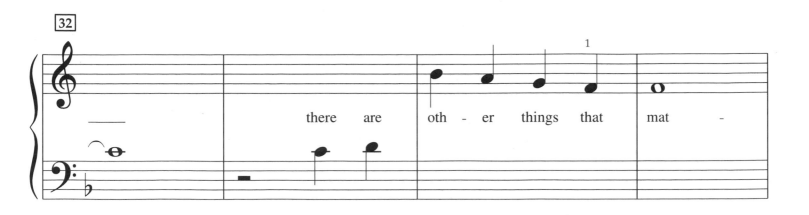

there are oth - er things that mat -

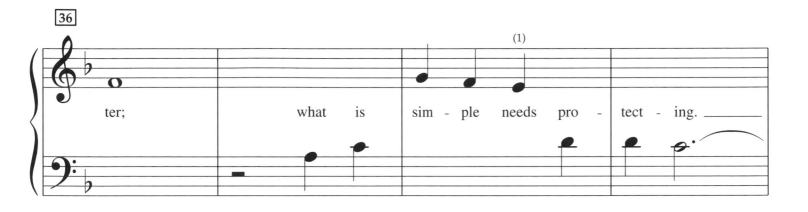

ter; what is sim - ple needs pro - tect - ing.

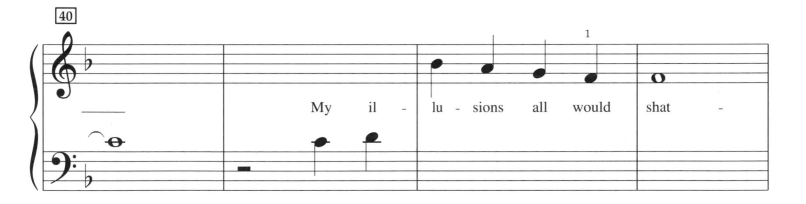

My il - lu - sions all would shat -

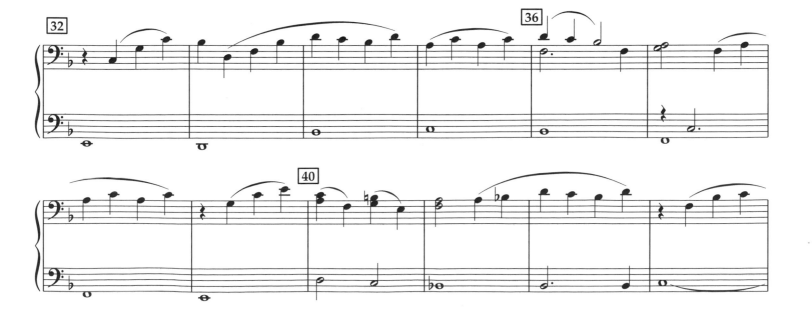

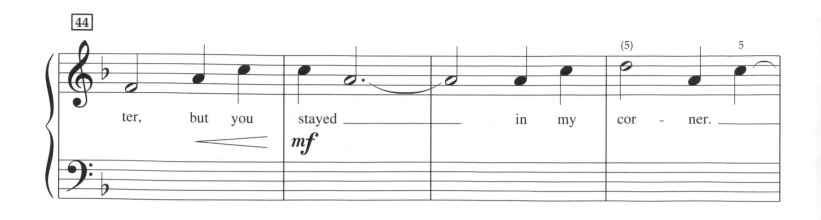

ter, but you stayed ____ in my cor - ner. ____

____ The on - ly world I knew was up - side ____

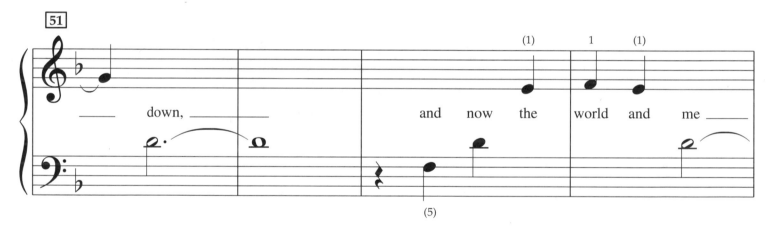

____ down, ____ and now the world and me ____

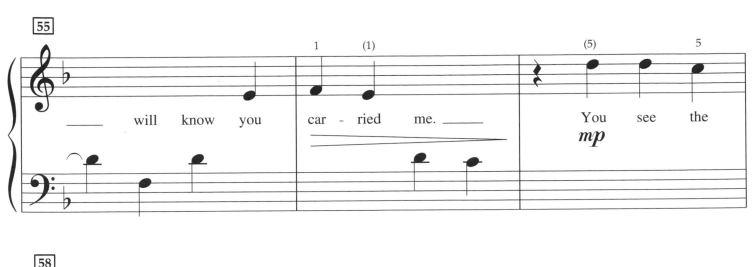

will know you car - ried me. _____ You see the
mp

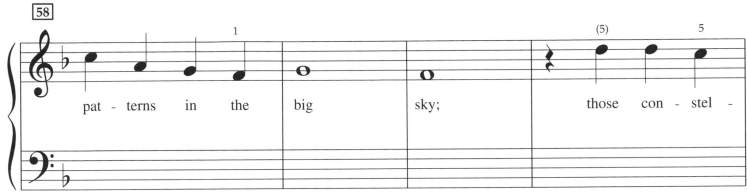

pat - terns in the big sky; those con - stel -

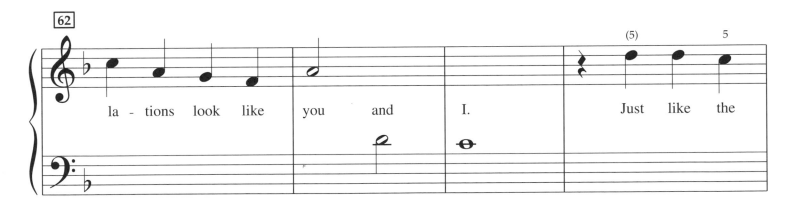

la - tions look like you and I. Just like the

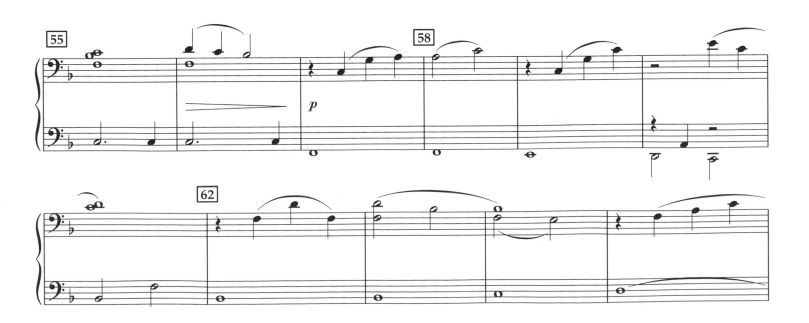

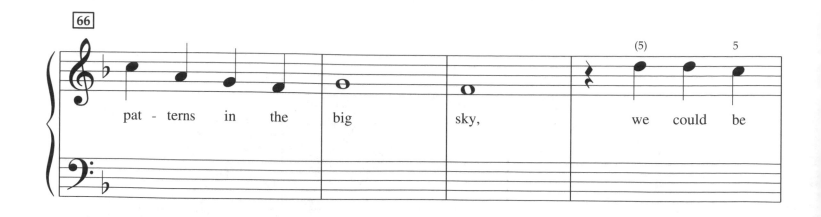

pat - terns in the big sky, we could be

lost; we could re - fuse to try. _____ But to have

cresc. *mf*

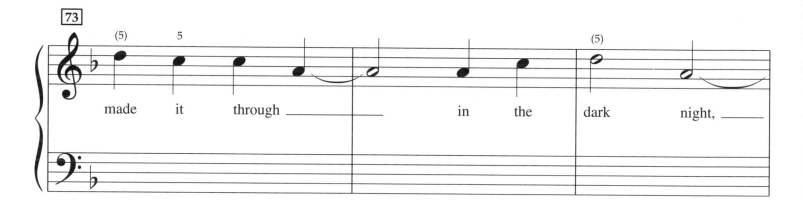

made it through _____ in the dark night, _____

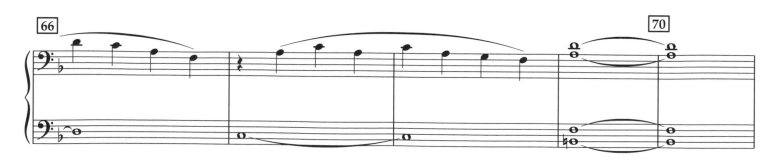

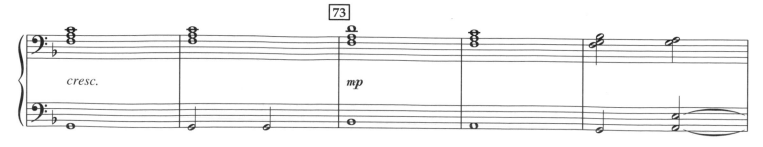

cresc. *mp*

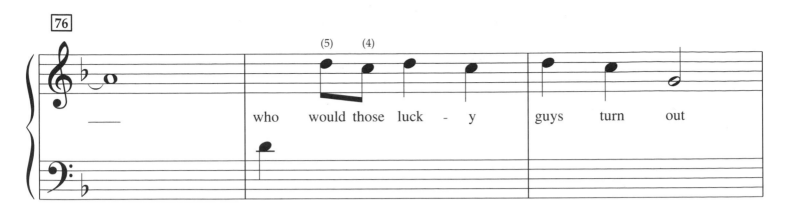

who would those luck - y guys turn out

to be _____ but that un - u - sual blend _____

mp

_____ of my fun - ny friend and me. _____

rit.

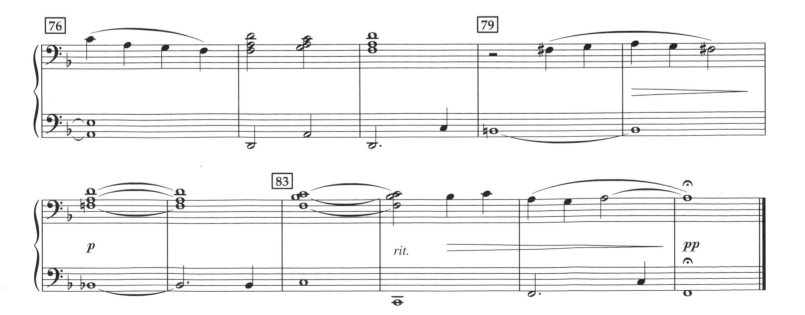

p

rit.

pp

Two Worlds
from Walt Disney Pictures' TARZAN™

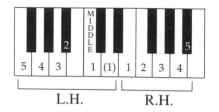

Words and Music by
Phil Collins

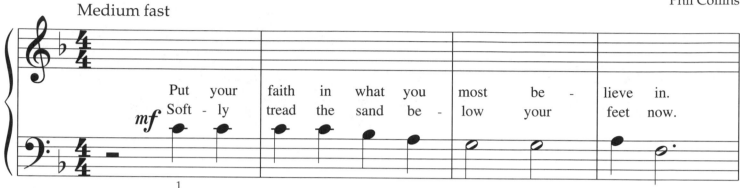

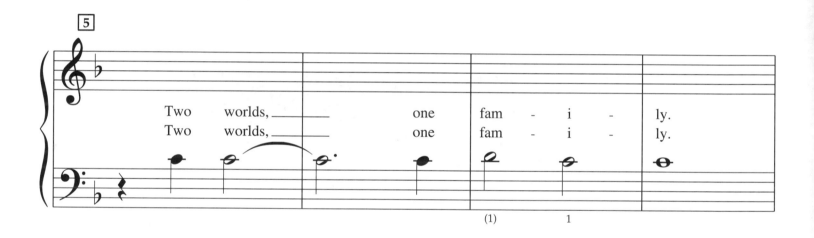

Duet Part (Student plays one octave higher than written.)

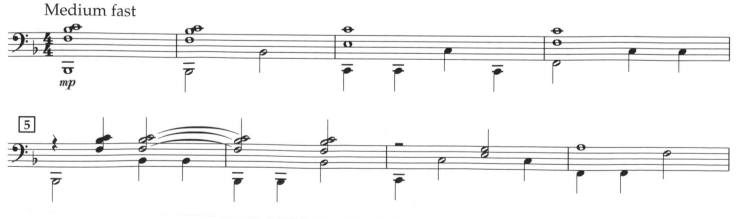

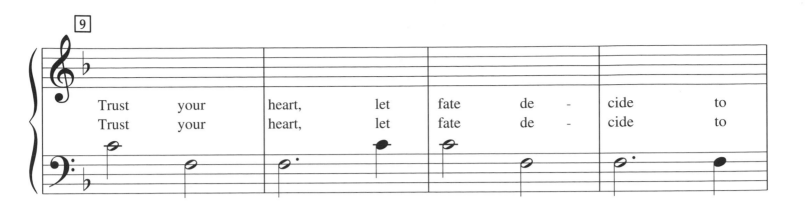

Trust your heart, let fate de - cide to
Trust your heart, let fate de - cide to

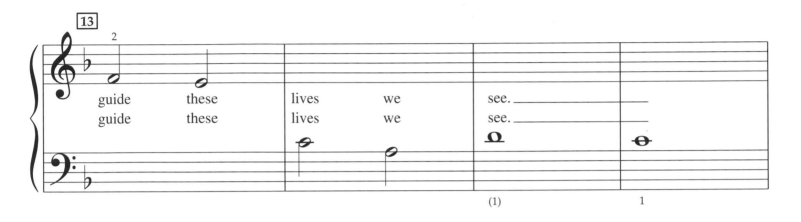

guide these lives we see.
guide these lives we see.

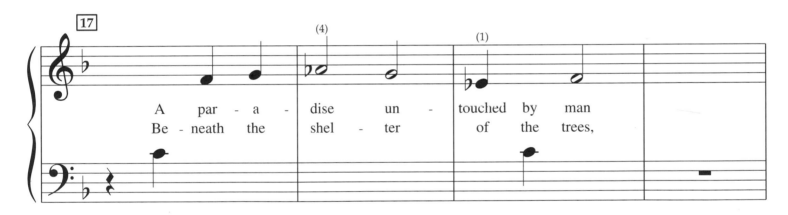

A par - a - dise un - touched by man
Be - neath the shel - ter of the trees,

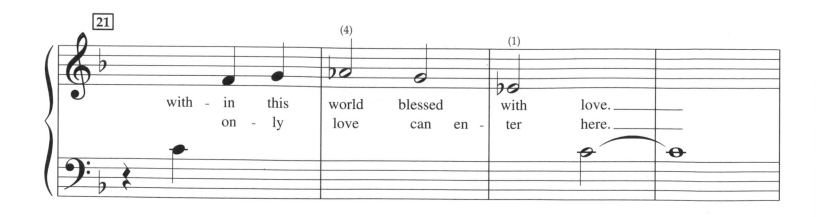

with - in this world blessed with love._____

on - ly love can en - ter here._____

A simple life they live in peace.

A simple life life they live in peace.

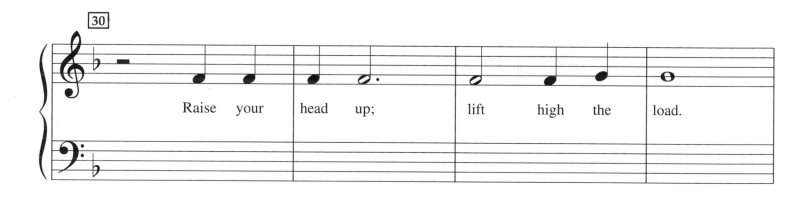

Raise your head up; lift high the load.

Take strength from those that need you. Build

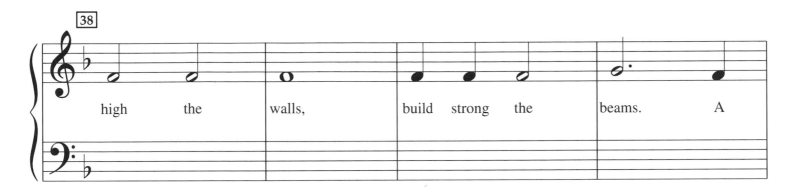

high the walls, build strong the beams. A

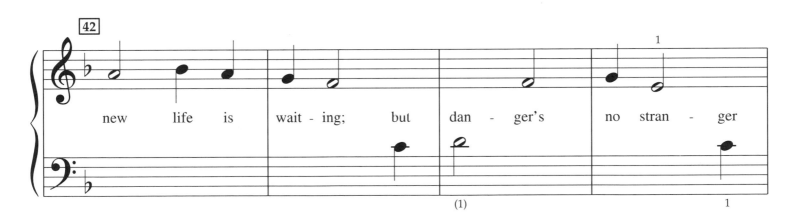

new life is wait-ing; but dan - ger's no stran - ger

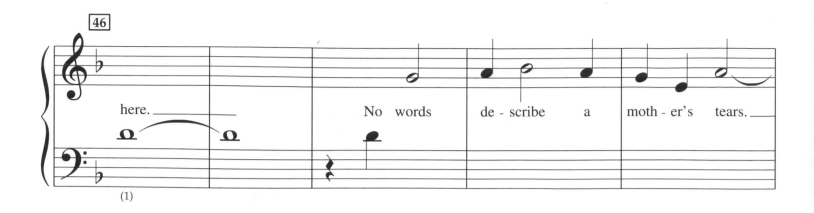

here._____ No words de - scribe a moth - er's tears.____

(1)

_____ No words can heal a bro - ken heart.

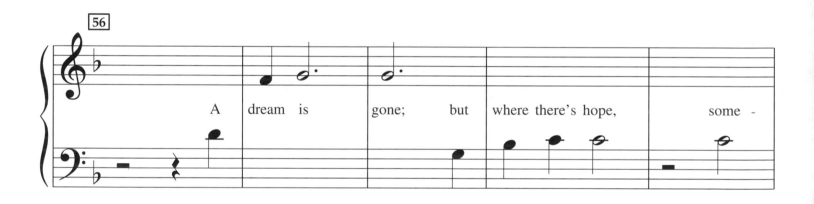

A dream is gone; but where there's hope, some -

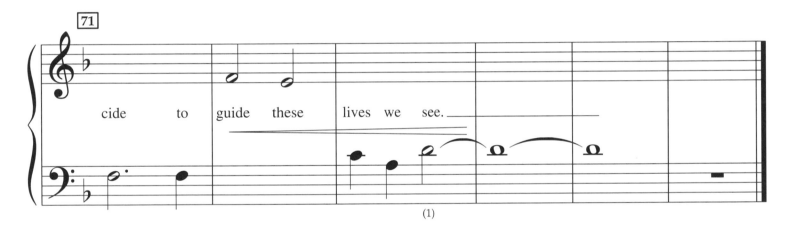

35

A Whole New World
from Walt Disney's ALADDIN

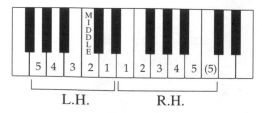

Music by Alan Menken
Lyrics by Tim Rice

Sweetly

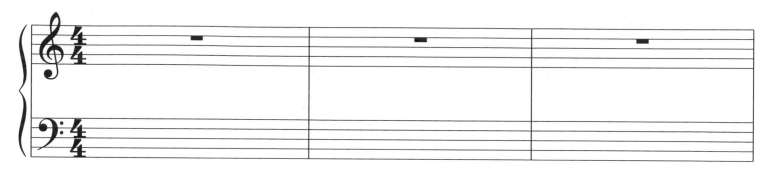

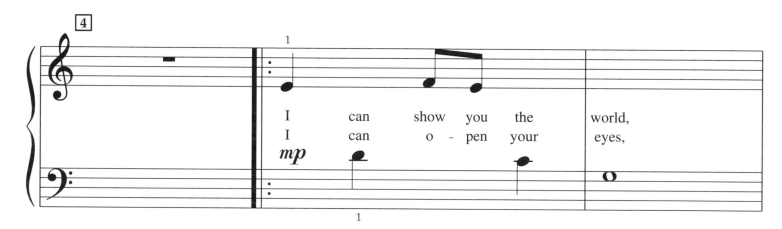

I can show you the world,
I can o - pen your eyes,

Duet Part (Student plays one octave higher than written.)

Sweetly

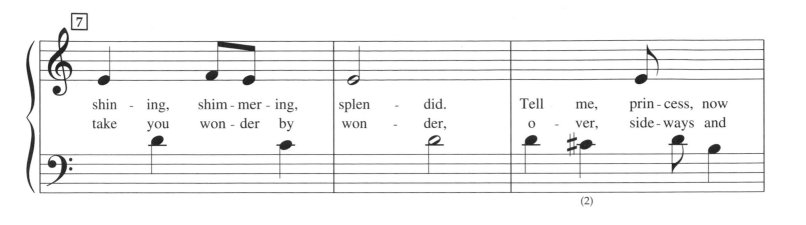

shin - ing, shim - mer - ing, splen - did.   Tell   me,   prin - cess, now
take   you   won - der by   won - der,   o - ver,   side - ways and

(2)

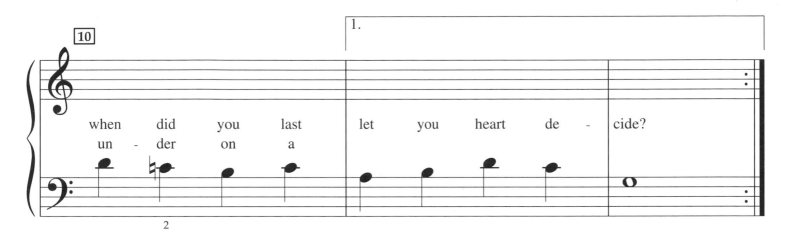

when   did   you   last   let   you   heart   de - cide?
un - der   on   a

1.

2

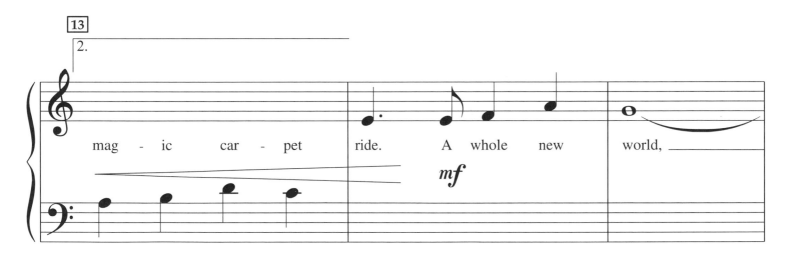

2.

mag - ic   car - pet   ride.   A   whole   new   world, _____

mf

mp

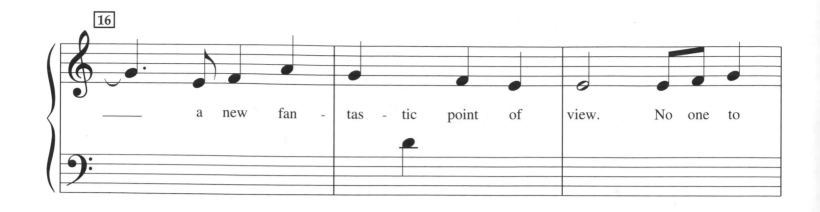

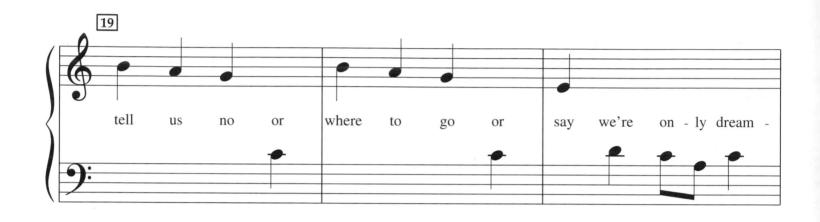

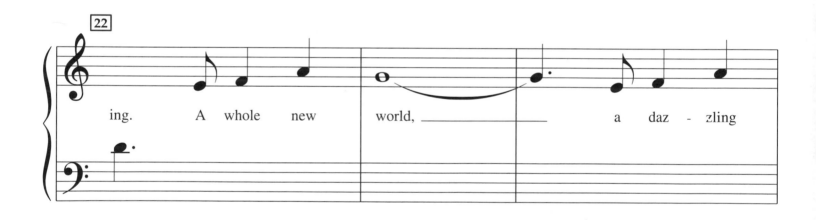

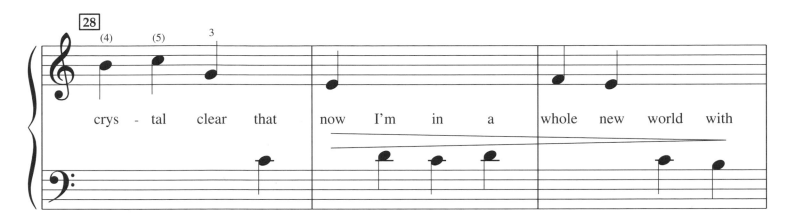

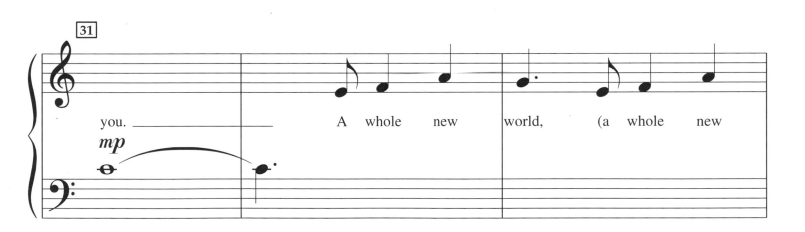

world,)   that's where we'll be (that's where we'll be.)   A thrill - ing

chase,   a won - d'rous place for you and me.

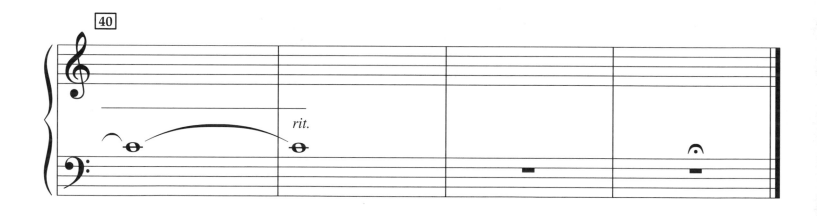

40

Written in the Stars
from Walt Disney Theatrical Productions' AIDA

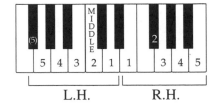

L.H.   R.H.

Music by Elton John
Lyrics by Tim Rice

With expression

AIDA:

I am here to tell you we can nev - er meet a -

gain. Sim - ple real - ly, is - n't it? A

Duet Part (Student plays one octave higher than written.)

With expression

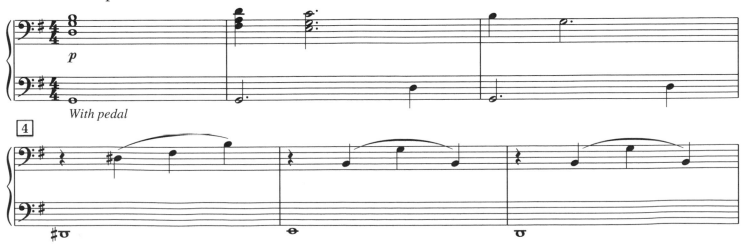

With pedal

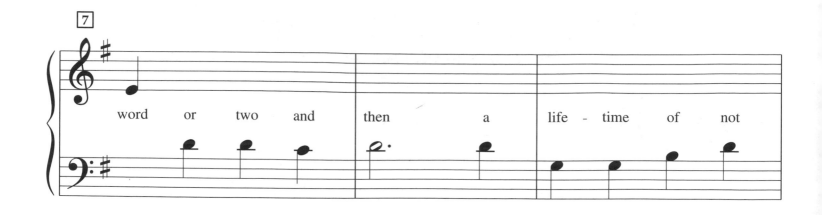

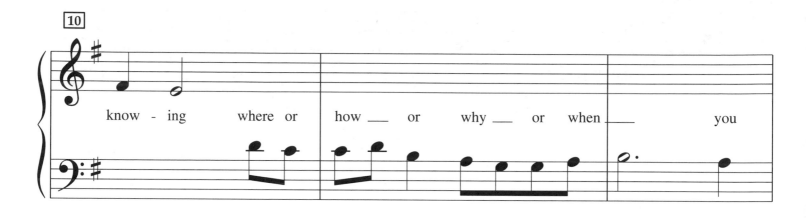

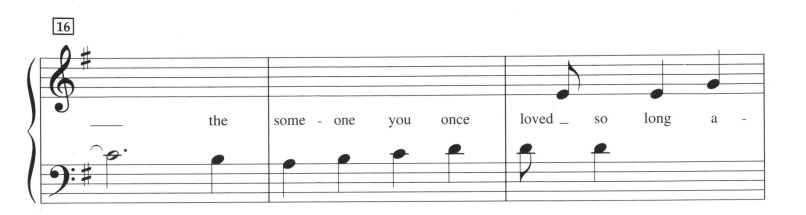

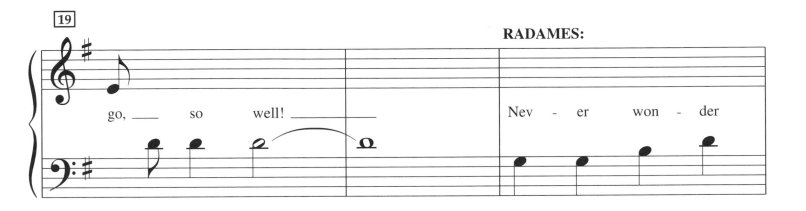

RADAMES:

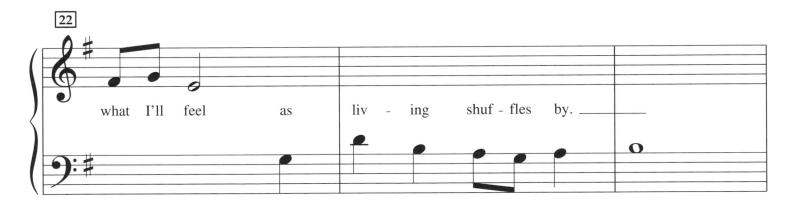

You don't have to ask me and I need not re - ply. ___

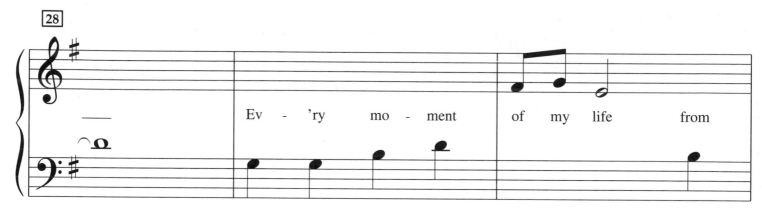

___ Ev - 'ry mo - ment of my life from

now un - til I die, ___ I will think or

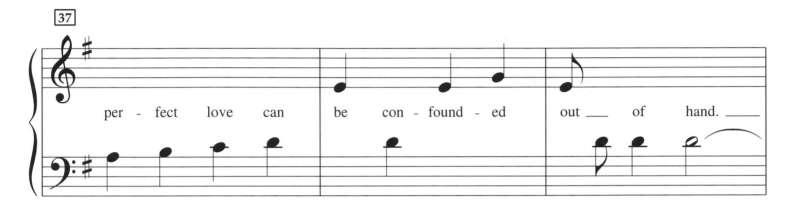

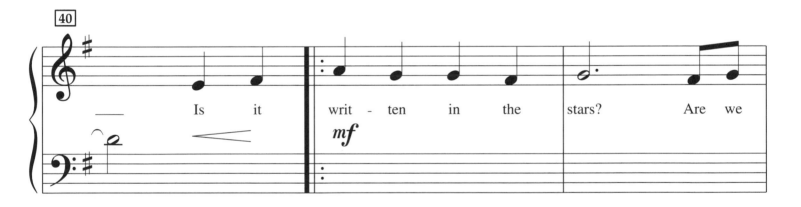

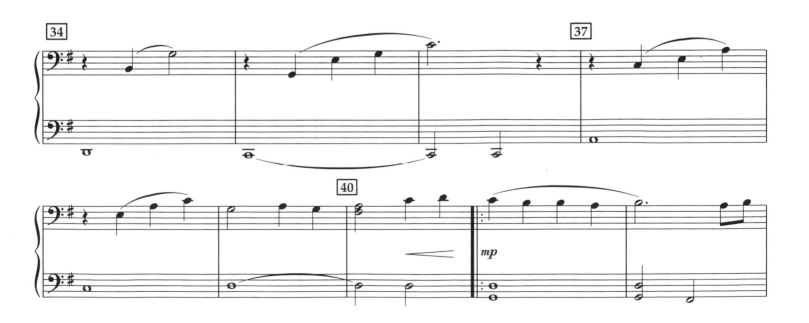

RADAMES & AIDA:

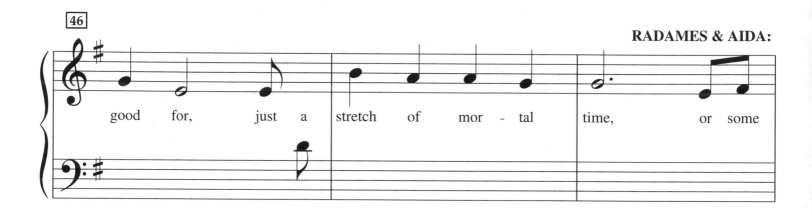

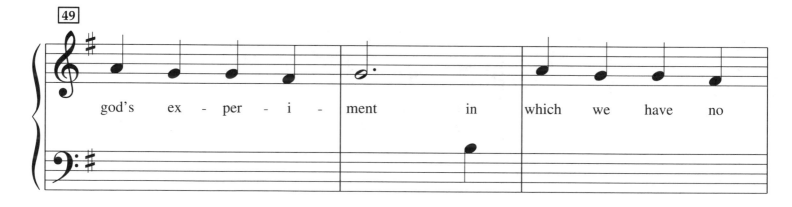

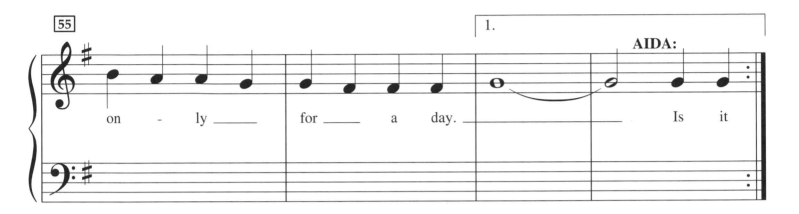

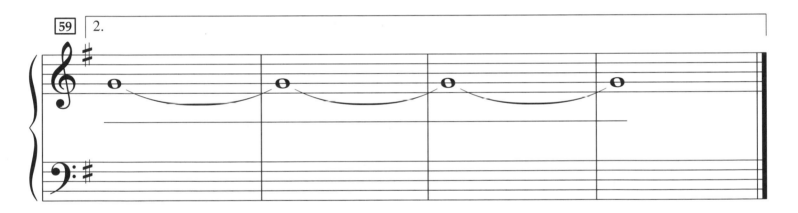

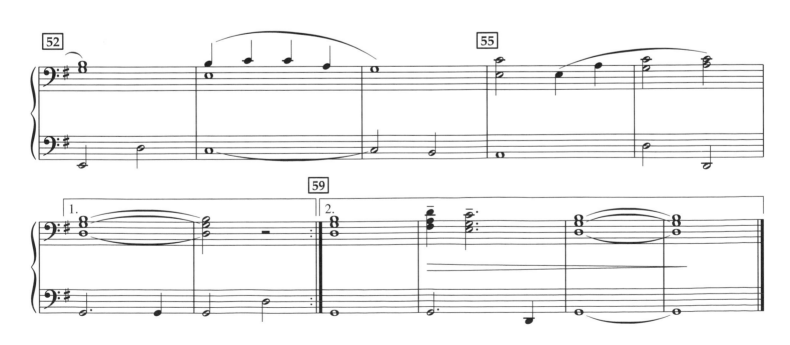